Scrapbooking Made Easy

Terrific Titles:
Getting Off to a Great Start

To Teri—the cutest redhead in Idaho—now that's a title!

Jill A. Rinner

introduction

Picture the Academy Awards. It's the final award and everyone awaits breathlessly for its announcement. The ever-chic, slender celebrity smiles and states, "And the winner for Best Picture goes to . . . (envelope ripping) . . . the story about the boat that sank in cold ocean waters after hitting an iceberg!" Ha!?!

What's in a title? And where would we be without them? These are some of the questions we will answer in this book. I will show you how a title does make a difference, how to choose one, where to place it, and all you need to know to make those title pages extra special!

"hey, you!"

We all have titles, whether we want to admit that or not. Our given names are a title. Just try calling your children without one ("hey, blond one!) or attempt to call a place of business and try to actually get the person you want to talk to on

It's always fun to look at pictures, especially if it is of some cute kid! But let's face it that can get boring real quick without the words to give it personality. It's like dating a guy that's really hot, but never says a word.

the phone ("yea, can I talk to the guy in that department that makes those things").

Titles are a good thing. They help us locate the video, song, or book we might be looking for. Without them, there would be chaos and a lot of wasted time trying to locate people or items we need. Titles actually give us direction.

Check out the difference in the sample page layouts below. What's missing in the first one? The colors and the photographs are the same, and the journaling seems to be in order. However, one crucial thing is different. You can see, without a title, the focus is gone.

The title sets the stage for the feeling of the story. Hoola Hoop and trampoline jumping may never be Olympic events, but it's always fun to dream. Who knows, maybe in the 2012 Olympics we may see some changes.

more power to ya!

If words give power, than a title can be the main muscle for any written prose. A title brings focus to your scrapbook page. In just a few short words, the entire feeling of an event can be summed up.

A Title Should Do One of 3 Things
1. Give information 2. Convey a feeling 3. Create interest

Let's go over each of these points. First, a title should **give information.** This could be as simple as "Boston 1988," "Fall Days 1996," or "First Haircut." When supplying information in a title, it is best to get right to the point and keep it simple.

When choosing to **convey a feeling** in the form of a title, many interesting words and phrases can be chosen. This can also be as simple as one word. For example, "Ouch!" "Super!" or "Mine!" immediately lead us to the feelings of something that hurt, a job well done or toddler selfishness among playmates. A feeling was created and the foundation set for the rest of the story to unfold.

Phrases can do the same, serving as the beginning of a story you wish to tell. "How Do I Love Thee . . ." "No Greater Joy . . ." or "Superstar Athlete!" are titles that beg for more information. The key is to keep the reader's interest through *wanting*. They *want* to know more, and you've got them hooked through the feeling!

This leads us to the third concept of **creating interest.** "Once upon a time . . ." has always been the classic opening for a story, but can also

A title can do all three things as shown here: give information, convey a feeling, and create interest. Holy Cow! Just a few words and you've changed the world (well. . . at least the layout.

serve as a title for a scrapbook page. With the title, you want to pique an interest. With just enough words to arouse your reader, you can add the excitement and intrigue in a title that will help create the focus of your layout and the basis for the story to come. "Holy Cow! I'm Getting My Ears Pierced!" was a title I used on a page about my daughter, that not only created a focus for the layout (cow print), gave information (getting ears pierced), conveyed a feeling (holy cow, the pain was a surprise!) and created interest to want to read on and hear the rest of the story.

While remembering these three points, you can easily choose titles to give your scrapbook pages the focus they need. Although you may

OUR FIRST WINTER

After a lifetime in Southern California, Mom and Dad spent their first real winter in Salt Lake City, Utah in December 1997. At last, an excuse to buy more winter clothes!

There's a first time for everything, no matter how old you are! So, you've had your last time to make a page without a title. A title creates the focus need- ed to recall a special memory of the past.

find some ideas to inspire you in books that give you title samples, you will not need to be dependent on someone else's title version of an event. Draw upon your memory with these simple three points, and choose a title that will fascinate your reader into wanting to know more about your wonderful memories!

To decide which of these three points is best for your layout, ask yourself this question: **What was the most important part of the memory?** Just the fact of what it was? Go with an information title. Was it the feeling? Then convey that feeling through the title. Did something interesting or out of the ordinary happen? Then use your title to create that interest.

give it a title

If you don't give it a title, someone else will! And it may be . . . BORING! While reading information located on a scrapbook page (hopefully the who, what, where, and why of what happened), the person examining your pictures and journaling may draw their own conclusion as to what the event was about.

Going to the dentist can be pretty boring (no offense, Dr. Watts). So give your page a title that will give the same shock your mother had when she found out you had eight cavities! There goes the scrapbooking budget for the month.

On Lizzy's first trip to the dentist, in July 1998, he discovered she had 8 cavities! 4 visits and $800 later...but she was very brave!

Now, I realize this may not seem like a life or death situation, but you can be darn sure that if I take the time to scrapbook a memory from my life, I want the correct information given, feeling and all! Remember, scrapbooking is a personal history and should be as accurate as possible. So unless you have the pictures and the tattoo to prove it, no one is going to buy the fact that you may have had a short fling in college with Harrison Ford.

everybody needs somebody

I f everybody needs somebody, then titles and journaling are a couple. Giving a title is only half the story, and should not be an excuse for not adding the most important words to your pictures…the photo journaling. Although a great title can give information and bring about feeling as stated before, it is the details of your pictures that make the true difference. The who and when are particularly important for establishing the historical facts of a photograph.

Use your title to begin telling the story of the memory. In *Photo Journaling: Telling the Story* (also in this booklet series) we discuss creative ways to give information to your pictures. The title you choose acts as the jumping off point for your storytelling.

Even mundane activities, like having a piano delivered, can be exciting with the right title and layout. Titles bring excitement to your page, so let the scrap-booking begin!

high and low

If you are now wondering where to find titles, your search is over. There are many places to find inspiration for titles and just down right copy them. A few good places to go to steal titles for scrapbook pages are the following:

Video Store—need I say more? Who has more titles than these people?

Movie Guide Book—like to steal your titles in private? A small investment can be made in a book that lists every movie title ever made. Most of these are paperback and very inexpensive.

Book Store—why reinvent the wheel? Walk the aisle of the subject you are scrapbooking (garden, babies, etc.) and get plenty of ideas for your pages. Don't forget your notepad or Dictaphone.

TV Guide—same as a movie guide with new ideas weekly!

Thesaurus—look up a word that has something to do with the event and find more gratifying and fulfilling words for title use (see, I use mine too!)

Don't fall over from exhaustion trying to find the right title for your page. It can be as easy as one descriptive word that can sum up the event, PRONTO!

Title Idea Books—these books have been compiled with you in mind. Usually laid out with themes, titles, quotes and scriptures, they are organized in a handy reference guide format.

Music—check out your CD collection or think of your favorite lullaby or hymn for title and/or phrase ideas.

Your Brain—I know this sounds like a long stretch, but thinking of the memory may actually make something pop into your head! Wouldn't that be cool?!

*If you need some additional help finding inspiration, refer to *Finding Inspiration: Defining Your Personal Style,* also in this book series.

There's no fun like title fun. And scrapbookers "just wanna have fun." Input some enthusiasm into your titles with a few words that rhyme.

where to put it

Now that you have come up with your title, where does it go? A title can be displayed many different ways on your page. It will add, not only real content, but visual interest to your layout, as well. It can be executed many ways, but let's cover effective placement.

When using background paper, a title can be placed on a solid piece of paper so that it doesn't get lost in the pattern of the paper. Here, the title box is made into a chalkboard in keeping with the school theme.

Single Page Layout Ideas

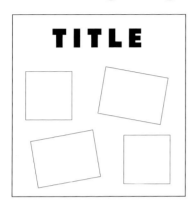 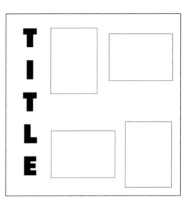

A title can be placed many different ways on your layout, just make sure

1. It's large enough to be noticed immediately
2. No words are misspelled, unless on purpose for emphasis
3. It's legible (I didn't say perfect, just legible).

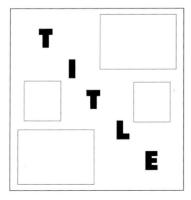 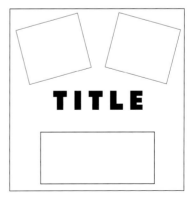

Single Page Layout Ideas (cont'd)

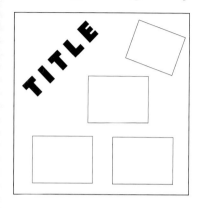 

Titles can be made from
1. Creative lettering by your own hand
2. Sticker letters or phrases
3. Traced with an alphabet template directly on paper
   or onto different paper and then cut out.

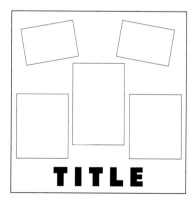 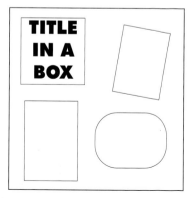

Double Page Layout Ideas

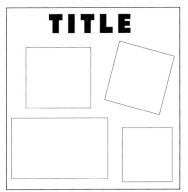 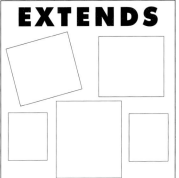

These two types of titles (extending across two pages) draw your eye out and across the layout, hinting that there must be more to look at. Consequently, these are good for layouts of more than just two pages.

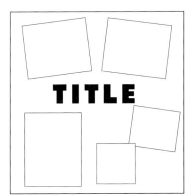 

Double Page Layout Ideas (cont'd)

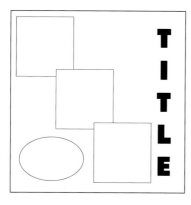 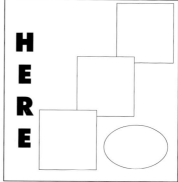

These two samples are best if your layout only consists of two pages. The one above keeps your eye pulled inward while the one below hints that "this is it" with the title at the beginning and continuing until the end of the layout.

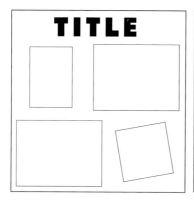 

Of course, titles do not have to be placed straight to be effective. In fact, that can be dull. Add visual emphasis by placing titles

- **On a curved line**
- **Within a shape**
- **With letters scattered or jumping**
- **Surrounded by matting**
- **Individual letters or words on die cut shapes**
- **Bordering a page**

Use creative lettering whenever possible. This makes the title even that much more personal when it is written by your own hand.

subtitles

Subtitles are a secondary title, used within a scrapbook layout segment of a particular event of more than three pages, that can explain or highlight a change in the activity. The easiest way to explain this is to show you. The samples shown on the following pages are the entire layout for a trip to the Bahamas. You may have seen a few of these pages published before, but they were shown by themselves and out of context. You can see, when compiled together, each segment changes with a new subtitle, emphasizing a new activity. Although "Bahamas" is the title that could umbrella the entire story, the subtitles bring new meaning to each arrangement of photos.

Subtitles are best used when scrapbooking an event that will stretch out among several pages. They can be classified with a new activity, a change in feeling or setting, or a switch in location.

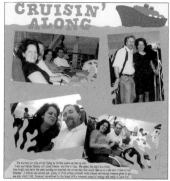

the 3 c's of choosing a title

Creates **Focus**
Gives information about the event
Shares a feeling that remains with the memory
Creates more interest for a particular recollection

Captures **Attention**
With interesting placement on your page
Through proper execution for the layout, taking into account
how many pages there will be in total
By using variety (it is the spice of life!) in placement, execution
and content

Communicates **with the Right Words and Phrases**
Subtitles—used to define a change in activity or feeling
Journaling—gives more details of the story
Closing Comments—wraps up the feelings of an event in a few
words or less

Choose a title that will make a statement about the story you are
telling. A title will be your chance to make a first impression, to plant
a thought, and to help that memory come to life. Remember . . . create, capture, and communicate your feelings through a chosen title.

frankly my dear . . .

E very good scrapbook story deserves a great beginning and an even better ending. Actually, so does every book, (so I'm sweating it out here to come up with something fabulous for my closing!). Don't forget to add those special words at the end of a layout that could encircle all the feelings exhibited within the memory.

Thomas Jefferson once stated, "Frankly my dear . . ."—oops! Wrong quote. He didn't say that, but I believe he did say, "The ultimate power lies in the people themselves. If you think them not enlightened to cast an informed discretion, the remedy is not to take away their discretion . . . but simply inform it." Consider yourself informed, and get to work! A great title will be the essence of getting off to a great start!

About the Author

Jill Rinner is a nationally recognized authority on scrapbooking. She has taught hundreds of classes about the many facets of scrapbooking—from the basics to advanced, creative lettering and much more. Jill is a frequent contributor to *Creating Keepsakes*™ magazine.

Photo taken in Cape Cod, MA.

When she is not scrapbooking, Jill loves to spend time with her husband and their three children. She also enjoys gardening, traveling, organizing and reading. Jill lives in Okemos, Michigan, where she is the co-owner of a fabulous scrapbook store called Our Favorite Things.